Programming Logic for AI: Introduction to Programming with a Focus on Artificial Intelligence

Summary

1. Introduction
2. Fundamentals of Programming Logic
3. Computational Thinking for AI
4. Data Structures and Algorithms
5. Classical Algorithms for AI
6. Introduction to Machine Learning
7. Data Manipulation for AI
8. Creating a Simple AI Model
9. Debugging and Logic Practices in AI
10. Conclusion and Next Steps

Chapter 1: Introduction

Objective: To present the content and importance of programming logic for AI development.

- **Introduction to AI**: Basic concept, how AI is transforming the world and areas where it is applied.
- **Why learn programming logic for AI?** Explain the importance of logic and how it is used to solve complex problems.

Chapter 2: Fundamentals of Programming Logic

Objective: To introduce the reader to the basics of programming logic, essential for any AI project.

- **Variables and Operators:** Types of data (integers, strings, booleans), variables, and mathematical and logical operators.
- **Conditional Structures:** Explain if, else, and switch, with Python code examples.
    - *Example:* A program that checks if a person is of legal age.
- **Repetition Structures:** Explain for, while, and the importance of repetitions in AI.
    - *Example:* Loop that averages a list of grades.
- **Practical Exercise:** Create a pseudocode program that checks the even numbers in a list.

Chapter 3: Computational Thinking for AI

Objective: To develop the ability to think logically and computationally to solve problems.

- **Problem Breakdown:** Breaking down large problems into smaller, easier-to-solve pieces.
- **Pattern Recognition:** How to identify patterns in data for building AI algorithms.
- **Abstraction and Algorithms:** Explain the importance of abstracting details to focus on the core logic.
- **Practical Exercise:** Create an algorithm that analyzes a sequence of numbers and identifies patterns (example of arithmetic progression).

Chapter 4: Data Structures and Algorithms

Objective: To teach essential data structures and basic algorithms, which serve as the basis for AI.

- **Lists, Stacks, and Queues**: Explanation with examples and use cases.
- **Dictionaries and Sets**: Useful data structures for manipulating large amounts of information.
- **Basic Algorithms**: Linear search, binary search, simple sorting.
- **Practical Exercise**: Write a program that finds the largest number in a list using a repeating structure.

Chapter 5: Classical Algorithms for AI

Objective: To introduce algorithms that are commonly used in AI and related areas.

- **Search and Sorting Algorithms**: Explain linear, binary, and sorting algorithms (bubble sort, quicksort).
- **Applications in AI**: Practical examples of how these algorithms are applied.
    - *Example*: Ordering data for analysis in machine learning models.
- **Practical Exercise**: Implement a sorting algorithm in Python.

Chapter 6: Introduction to Machine Learning

Objective: To provide an overview of machine learning and how it uses programming logic.

- **What is Machine Learning?** Explain supervision, non-supervision, and reinforcement learning.
- **Building a Simple Model**: Create a basic classification model with real examples.
    - *Example*: Classify fruits by size and color.
- **Practical Exercise**: Implement a simple classification model in Python.

Chapter 7: Data Manipulation for AI

Objective: To teach data manipulation, which is essential for pre-processing in AI.

- **Data Collection and Cleansing**: Introduce how to clean and organize data.
- **Python Libraries**: Explain the use of NumPy and Pandas for data manipulation.
- **Practical Exercise**: Load a simple dataset and organize it with Pandas.

Chapter 8: Creating a Simple AI Model

Objective: To guide the reader in creating a basic AI model using programming logic.

- **Defining the Problem and Data:** Identify the problem that the model will solve.
- **Model Development:** Write the code for a basic model.
    - *Example:* A simple binary classifier.
- **Practical Exercise:** Create a model that classifies simulated data using Python.

Chapter 9: Debugging and Logic Practices in AI

Objective: To teach how to find and fix errors in AI code.

- **Debugging:** Debugging techniques and tools in Python.
- **Logic Improvement:** How to optimize programming logic for performance.
- **Practical Exercise:** A code with intentional error for the reader to correct.

Chapter 10: Conclusion and Next Steps

Objective: To reinforce what has been learned and offer directions for continuous study.

- **Summary of Key Concepts:** Recap of the main concepts covered.
- **Next Steps:** Course recommendations, books, and resources to dive deeper.

- **Final Message**: Encouragement to continue exploring AI based on the knowledge gained.

Material Extra

- **Glossary**: Fundamental logic and AI terms and concepts.
- **References and Recommended Reading**: Links and books on programming logic and AI.
- **Code Examples: Ready-to-download codes in Python, for practical study.**

Formatting and Design Tips

- **Images and Diagrams**: Include flowcharts, data tables, and visualizations for easy understanding.
- **Highlighted Code**: Formatting code in clear, well-commented blocks.
- **Style**: Use accessible and relaxed language to make learning lighter.

This eBook will be a great introduction for anyone who wants to learn programming and logic with a focus on AI.

Chapter 1: Introduction

1.1. Artificial Intelligence (AI) Overview

This topic should provide an introduction to Artificial Intelligence and its importance in today's world.

- **Definition of AI**: Explain what Artificial Intelligence is. AI is the area of computer science dedicated to developing systems that can perform tasks that normally require human intelligence, such as speech recognition, computer vision, and decision-making.

- **AI Application Areas:**
    - **Health**: Diagnosis of diseases, analysis of exams and remote monitoring of patients.
    - **Industry and Automation**: Use of robots in production lines, process optimization and predictive maintenance.
    - **Finance**: Credit analysis algorithms, fraud detection, and automated trading.
    - **Customer Services**: Virtual assistants, chatbots, and product recommendations.

- **AI's Impact on the Labor Market and Society**: Address how AI is creating new job opportunities in areas such as data analytics, algorithm development, and AI ethics, as well as transforming traditional professions.

1.2. The Importance of Programming Logic for AI

Here, the goal is to explain the importance of programming logic as a foundation for understanding and developing artificial intelligence.

- **The Role of Logic in Problem Solving**: Programming logic allows for the creation of structured and efficient solutions. In AI, the ability to decompose complex problems into logical steps is critical to building robust algorithms.

- **Why Logic Matters for AI Models**:
    - **Structure and Implementation of Algorithms**: Many AI algorithms, such as neural networks, search algorithms, and supervised learning, rely on logic concepts.
    - **Decision Making**: Logic helps in programming systems capable of making rule-based decisions, which is a basis for creating machine learning models.
- **Practical Example**: Introduce a simple example of a system that, based on inputs, makes decisions — such as a program that identifies whether a person can vote according to age.

1.3. What to Expect from the E-book

- **General Objective**: This eBook will teach programming logic applied to AI by helping the reader develop the foundation for creating and understanding artificial intelligence models.
- **How the Book Is Structured**:
    - **Progressive Chapters**: Each chapter is designed to build a solid foundation, gradually advancing to more applied topics such as machine learning.
    - **Practical Examples and Exercises**: The book will bring code examples and practical exercises, especially in Python, to reinforce theoretical learning.

1.4. Requirements and Prerequisites

Clarify previous knowledge and recommended tools for the reader to better enjoy the content.

- **Basic Knowledge**: To follow this e-book, no advanced programming knowledge is required. It is suitable for beginners or those with little experience who want to familiarize themselves with the logic applied to AI.

- **Recommended Tools**: Python will be the primary language used in the examples, as it is widely used in AI. Suggest that the reader install Python and familiarize themselves with a code editor (such as Jupyter Notebook or Visual Studio Code).

- **Additional Resources**:
    - **Libraries**: Explain that throughout the e-book specific libraries will be used, such as NumPy and Pandas, which will be introduced gradually.
    - **Development Environment**: Recommend a basic setup, such as Anaconda for managing environments in Python, useful for those who are not familiar with installing packages.

1.5. Introduction to Python and Pseudocode

- **Python for AI**: Quickly introduce the Python language as the top language for AI development due to its simplicity and broad community.

- **Pseudocode**: Explain the importance of pseudocode for learning logic without initially worrying about the syntax of the language. Present a simple example of pseudocode and its translation into Python:
    - **Pseudocode**: Example of a program to check whether a number is odd or even.

    ```plaintext
    SE (número MOD 2 == 0)
        ENTÃO escreva "O número é par"
    SENÃO
        escreva "O número é ímpar"
    ```

- **Python**: Python code corresponding to the pseudocode above.

```plaintext
SE (número MOD 2 == 0)
    ENTÃO escreva "O número é par"
SENÃO
    escreva "O número é ímpar"
```

- **Practical Exercise**: Create a simple pseudocode program so that the reader better understands the importance of logic.

1.6. Motivation and Next Steps

The journey of learning programming logic and artificial intelligence is full of challenges and rewards. With the knowledge gained throughout this eBook, you now have the fundamental tools to venture into the world of programming and AI. Programming logic and building algorithms are crucial skills that will serve as the basis for all your future projects and innovations in this area.

Motivation: Remember that every great artificial intelligence expert started with a simple step. Curiosity and persistence are your best allies. By exploring and applying what you've learned, you'll discover new ways to solve problems and create impactful solutions. AI is an ever-evolving area, and its contribution can make a difference in various sectors, from healthcare to education and sustainability.

Next steps:

1. Practice: Practice is essential to consolidate your learning. Try solving programming problems on platforms like HackerRank, LeetCode, or Codewars. Not only will this help bolster your skills, but it will also prepare you for real-world situations.

2. Personal Projects: Start a personal project that uses the concepts you have learned. It can be a simple prediction model, a chatbot, or any other application that interests you. Hands-on experience is invaluable.

3. Continuous Learning: Continue your education. Consider online courses, workshops, or tutorials in specific areas of AI, such as machine learning, natural language processing, or neural networks. Resources like Coursera, edX, and Udacity offer a vast array of courses for all levels.

4. Community: Join online communities such as coding forums, LinkedIn groups, or hackathon events. Interacting with other enthusiasts and professionals can provide valuable new ideas and perspectives.

5. Tools and Libraries Exploration: Familiarize yourself with leading AI libraries such as TensorFlow, Keras, and Scikit-learn. These tools are critical for building advanced models and simplify many development processes.

Chapter 2: Fundamentals of Programming Logic

2.1. Introduction to Basic Concepts

This topic covers the core elements of programming logic, explaining how they serve as the basis for creating algorithms and programs.

- **What is Programming Logic?** Define programming logic as the set of instructions organized in a logical way to solve a specific problem. Programming is essentially a way of describing solutions using a set of rules and frameworks.

- **Pseudocode as a Planning Tool**: Explain the importance of pseudocode for planning logic before writing the final code. Give simple examples and encourage the reader to sketch their ideas using pseudocode before coding in Python.

2.2. Variables and Data Types

Introduce the most common variable concepts and data types in programming.

- **Variables**: Explain what a variable is (a "box" for storing values) and how to declare a variable in Python. Show examples of how to define variables and assign values:

```python
nome = "Maria"
idade = 25
altura = 1.70
```

- **Types of Data:**
    - **Integer** (int): Whole numbers, such as -1, 0, 5.

- **Floating**: Decimal numbers, such as 2.5 or 3.14.
- **String** (str): Strings of text, such as "Hello, world!".
- **Boolean**: Logical values, True or False, used in conditions.

- **Practice Exercise**: Create variables to store a person's name, age, and height, and print those values in the console.

2.3. Mathematical and Logical Operators

At this point, explain the operators that help manipulate data and create conditions.

- **Mathematical Operators:**
    - **Addition (+), Subtraction (-), Multiplication (*), Division (/).**
    - **Modulus (%)**: Returns the rest of the division between two numbers.
    - *Example*: Calculate the average of three numbers.

- **Logical Operators:**
    - **E**: Returns True if both conditions are true.
    - **OR**: Returns True if either condition is true.
    - **NOT**: Reverses the logical value.
    - *Example*: Create a condition that checks if an age is between 18 and 65 years old.

- **Practical Exercise**: Create a program that receives two numbers from the user and verifies that both are even.

2.4. Conditional Structures

Conditional frameworks are critical for decision-making in programs. Explain how to use them to create different paths in your code.

- **If and else structure**:
    - How the if condition works: if a condition is true, it executes a block of code; otherwise, it jumps to the next block.
    - **Example**: Checking if a person is of legal age.

```python
idade = int(input("Digite sua idade: "))
if idade >= 18:
    print("Você é maior de idade.")
else:
    print("Você é menor de idade.")
```

ELIF Structure:

- When we have multiple conditions, we can use elif to create more paths.
- **Example**: Check if a grade is sufficient for passing, retrieving, or failing.

```python
nota = float(input("Digite sua nota: "))
if nota >= 7.0:
    print("Aprovado")
elif nota >= 5.0:
    print("Recuperação")
else:
    print("Reprovado")
```

- **Practical Exercise**: Write a program that asks the user their age and, depending on their age, prints a different message (e.g., minor, adult, or elderly).

2.5. Repetition Structures

Repetition frameworks allow blocks of code to be executed multiple times, which are essential for data manipulation in AI.

- **Loop for:**
    - Explain the for loop in Python, which is used to iterate over sequences.
    - **Example**: Iterate over a list of numbers and print each one.

```python
numeros = [1, 2, 3, 4, 5]
for numero in numeros:
    print(numero)
```

Laço while:

- Explain the while loop, which keeps repeating as long as a condition is true.
- **Example**: Use while to count to 10.

```python
contador = 1
while contador <= 10:
    print(contador)
    contador += 1
```

- **Practical Exercise**: Create a program that asks the user to enter a password and repeats the request until the correct password is entered.

2.6. Functions: Modularizing the Code

Teach how to create functions to organize code into reusable blocks.

- **What is a Function?**: Functions allow you to group a set of instructions into a "box", which can be called whenever needed.
- **Defining Functions in Python**:
    - Syntax of a function: def nome_funcao():
    - **Example**: Function to display a welcome message.

```python
def boas_vindas():
    print("Bem-vindo ao sistema!")
```

Functions with Parameters:

- Explain how to pass information to a function and return values.
- **Example**: Function to add two numbers

```python
def soma(a, b):
    return a + b
resultado = soma(3, 5)
print(resultado)
```

- **Practical Exercise**: Create a function that takes a number and returns whether it is odd or even.

2.7. Practical Exercises and Problem Solving

End the chapter with practical exercises that help consolidate learning.

1. **Conditional Exercise**: Write a program that asks for a score from 0 to 10 and returns whether the score is "low" (0-5), "medium" (5-7), or "high" (7-10).
2. **Lasso for Exercise**: Create a program that takes a list of numbers and calculates the average.
3. **Exercise with Functions**: Write a function that takes two numbers and returns the larger one between them.
4. **Integration Exercise**: Ask the user to enter a list of integers. Using for, if, and functions, create a function that shows how many numbers are even and how many are odd.

2.8. Conclusion of the Chapter

Chapter 2 explored programming logic and the construction of algorithms, fundamental concepts that are the backbone of any development in artificial intelligence. Programming logic is essential for understanding how to solve problems in a structured and effective way, allowing programmers to translate real-world problems into computational solutions.

In this chapter, readers learned about the importance of representing algorithms clearly, using flowcharts and pseudocode. These methods not only make it easier to plan solutions but also help in communicating complex ideas in an accessible way. The introduction to the concept of algorithms, including their definition and characteristics, has provided a solid foundation for understanding how different approaches can be utilized to solve specific problems.

In addition, the discussion of basic operations and control structures provided practical tools that can be applied in a variety of programming scenarios. The examples and practical exercises helped consolidate this knowledge, allowing readers to develop their own skills in building algorithms.

With the understanding gained in this chapter, readers are well prepared to advance to the next level, where we will explore the essential data structures and algorithms that are indispensable for data manipulation and analysis in artificial intelligence projects. This progression will ensure that readers are equipped with the skills they need to tackle the most complex AI challenges.

Chapter 3: Data Structures and Data Manipulation

3.1. Introduction to Data Structures

This topic introduces the concept of data structures, explaining the importance of organizing data efficiently.

- **What Are Data Structures?** Explain that data structures are specialized formats for storing and organizing information, allowing data to be accessed and manipulated efficiently.
- **Importance for AI:** In artificial intelligence, dealing with large volumes of data is common. Data structures help organize and process this information quickly, and are essential for the performance of algorithms.

3.2. Lists

Start by introducing lists, one of the most basic and widely used frameworks in Python.

- **What is a List?** Explain that lists are ordered collections of elements that can be modified. They allow you to store various types of data, such as numbers and strings.
- **Basic Operations with Lists**:
    - **Creating a List**: *numbers = [1, 2, 3, 4, 5]*
    - **Accessing Elements**: *Numbers[0] (first element)*
    - **Modifying Elements**: *numbers[2] = 10*
    - **Adding and Removing Elements**: *numbers.append(6), numbers.remove(10)*
- **Practical Example**: Create a list of names and print a custom message for each name using a for loop.

- **Practical Exercise**: Create a program that receives a list of numbers and calculates the sum of all the elements.

3.3. Tuples

Tuples are similar to lists, but they are immutable, which makes them useful for storing data that should not be changed.

- **What is a Tuple?** A tuple is a sequence of elements that cannot be modified after it has been created.
- **Tuple Example**: *Coordinates = (10, 20)*
- **Advantages of Tuples**: Tuples are more efficient in terms of performance and are used to represent data that must remain constant.
- **Practical Example**: Create a tuple to represent a date (day, month, year) and print each element separately.

3.4. Dictionaries

Dictionaries are data structures that store key and value pairs, and are useful for representing information in an organized manner.

- **What is a Dictionary?** Dictionaries store data using key and value pairs. They are used to represent data in an associative way, such as a contact book.
- **Creating and Manipulating Dictionaries**:
    - **Example Dictionary**: *contact = {'name': 'John', 'age': 25, 'phone': '1234-5678'}*
    - **Accessing Values**: *contact['name']*
    - **Adding and Removing Items**: *contact['email'] = 'joao@email.com', del contact['phone']*
- **Practical Example**: Create a dictionary to store a student's information (name, age, course) and print this information.

- **Practical Exercise:** Create a dictionary to represent a product (name, price, quantity in stock) and implement a program that calculates the total value of the inventory.

3.5. Sets

Sets are data structures that store single elements, in no particular order.

- **What is a Set?** Sets store single elements and are used for operations such as join and intersect.
- **Creating and Manipulating Sets:**
    - **Set Example:** *numbers = {1, 2, 3, 4}*
    - **Operations with Sets:**
        - **Union:** *A | B*
        - **Intersection:** *A&B*
        - **Difference:** *A - B*
- **Practical Example:** Create two sets of numbers and show the union and intersection between them.
- **Practical Exercise:** Given a list of names with repetitions, create a set with the unique names and display them.

3.6. Data Manipulation with List Comprehension

List comprehensions are a concise and efficient way to create and manipulate lists in Python.

- **What is List Comprehension?:** List comprehension is a way to generate lists in a single line of code, facilitating data filtering and transformation operations.
- **Basic syntax:**

- - **Example**: squares = [x**2 for x in range(10)] (list of squares of numbers 0 to 9)
- **Practical Example**: Create a list of even numbers from 0 to 20 using list comprehension.
- **Practical Exercise**: Using list comprehension, create a list containing the names of an original list that begin with a certain letter.

3.7. Aggregation Functions and Basic Statistics

Teach how to calculate basic statistics, such as average and sum, using lists.

- **Aggregation Functions:**
  - **Soma**: sum(list)
  - **Highest and Lowest Value**: max(list), min(list)
  - **List Length**: len(list)
- **Basic Stats:**
  - **Media**: sum(list) / len(list)
- **Practical Example**: Calculate the average of an age list of a group of people.
- **Practical Exercise**: Create a list of temperatures recorded in a week and find the highest, lowest and average of the temperatures.

3.8. String Manipulation

Teach how to work with strings, including common text manipulation operations.

- **Basic String Operations:**
  - **Concatenation**: nome_completo = first name + " " + last name
  - **Slicing**: text[0:5]

- - **String Methods**: text.lower(), text.upper(), text.replace('a', 'e')
- **Practical Example**: Receive a user's full name and display the name in uppercase, lowercase, and capitalized.
- **Practical Exercise**: Receive a sentence from the user and count how many words there are in that sentence.

3.9. Practical Integration Exercises

Propose exercises that integrate the use of the data structures presented in this chapter.

1. **Contact Manager**: Create a dictionary where the keys are people's names and the values are the phones. Allow the user to add, edit, and remove contacts.
2. **Sales Report**: Create a program that stores products in a dictionary, where each key is the name of the product and the amount is the total sales. Allow the user to add sales and calculate the total sales at the end.
3. **Operations with Sets**: Create two sets with fruit names and find which fruits are in both sets, which are only in the first set, and which are only in the second.

3.10. Conclusion of the Chapter

Chapter 3 introduced the basic concepts of programming that are essential for building artificial intelligence systems. By exploring programming logic, variables, conditional structures, loops, and functions, readers were introduced to the fundamental tools that will enable the implementation of AI algorithms and models.

Understanding the logic behind programming is crucial for developing solutions that can solve complex problems. Conditional structures and loops, for example, are critical for decision-making and iteration in processes that involve large data sets. In addition, the introduction to functions promoted modularity and code reuse, principles that are vital in larger-scale programming projects.

This chapter also included practical exercises that helped reinforce learning by allowing readers to apply the theory concretely. By the end of this chapter, readers have a solid understanding of the basic principles of programming, preparing them for the next step in their journey: exploring data structures and algorithms that are crucial to artificial intelligence. This logical progression ensures that they are well-equipped to handle the more complex challenges that will come as they deepen their knowledge of AI.

Chapter 4: Algorithms and Control Structures

4.1. What is an Algorithm?

In this topic, introduce the concept of algorithm and its importance in programming and AI.

- **Definition of Algorithm**: Explain that an algorithm is a sequence of instructions to solve a specific problem. Each step of the algorithm must be clear and executable in a finite time.
- **Importance of Algorithms for AI**: Algorithms are fundamental in AI, as they allow you to process data, make decisions, and solve complex problems.
- **Example**: Demonstrate a simple algorithm for averaging three numbers.

4.2. Sequential, Conditional and Repetition Structures

Introduce the three main control structures used in algorithms: sequence, selection, and repetition.

- **Sequential Structures**: Explain how the sequential execution of instructions is the basis of any program, with commands being executed in a specific order.
- **Conditional Structures (Selection):**
    - **If-Else**: Show how to create conditions using if, else, and elif.
    - **Example**: Determining whether a person is of legal age based on their age.

```python
idade = int(input("Digite sua idade: "))
if idade >= 18:
    print("Maior de idade")
else:
    print("Menor de idade")
```

- **Repetition Structures (Loops):**
    - **For** and **While**: Explain how to use for to iterate over sequences and while to repeat a block of code as long as a condition is true.
    - **Example**: Use a for loop to sum all the numbers in a list, and a while loop to simulate a counter up to a specific number.

4.3. Structure and Representation of Algorithms

Explain how to construct and represent algorithms using flowcharts and pseudocode.

- **Pseudocode**: Describe pseudocode as a tool for planning algorithms before implementing actual code. Show basic examples, such as pseudocode to square a number.
- **Flow Charts**:
    - Introduce the use of flowcharts to visually represent the control flow of algorithms.
    - **Flowchart Example**: Create a simple flowchart to decide if a number is odd or even.
- **Practical Exercise**: Ask the reader to draw a flowchart and write pseudocode to determine if a number is positive, negative, or zero.

4.4. Sorting Algorithms

Introduce sorting algorithms, such as Bubble Sort, to teach the reader about data organization.

- **Bubble Sort:**
    - Explain how Bubble Sort works as a basic sorting algorithm that compares and swaps adjacent elements.
    - **Example**: Sort a list of numbers in ascending order using Bubble Sort.
- **Other Sorting Algorithms**:
    - Mention other algorithms, such as Selection Sort and Insertion Sort, highlighting that more advanced algorithms (such as Quick Sort and Merge Sort) are used in AI to manipulate large volumes of data.
- **Practical Exercise**: Implement Bubble Sort in Python to sort a user-provided list of numbers.

4.5. Search Algorithms

Explain search algorithms such as Linear Search and Binary Search, which are used to locate elements in a collection of data.

- **Busca Linear:**
    - Linear Search cycles through each element of a list until it finds the desired value.
    - **Example**: Write a linear search function that finds a specific number in a list.
- **Binary Search:**
    - Binary Search is a more efficient algorithm for ordered lists, which divides the list into parts and reduces the number of comparisons.

- **Example**: Demonstrate Binary Search to find an element in an ordered list.
- **Practical Exercise**: Implement a linear search and a binary search for a number in a list of integers and compare the efficiency of the two methods.

4.6. Recursive algorithms

Introduce recursion as an important technique for solving problems by breaking them down into smaller subproblems.

- **What is Recursion?**: Explain recursion as the technique where a function calls itself to solve a problem.
- **Recursion Example**: Calculate the factorial of a number using a recursive function.

```python
def fatorial(n):
    if n == 0:
        return 1
    else:
        return n * fatorial(n - 1)
```

- **Application in AI**: Discuss how recursion is used in AI to solve complex problems, such as in search algorithms and decision trees.
- **Practical Exercise**: Create a recursive function to calculate the factorial of a number and a function to calculate the Fibonacci sequence.

4.7. Advanced Control Structures: Lambda, Map, Filter, and Reduce Functions

Introduce functional functions and operations in Python, which are useful for processing data in AI.

- **Lambda functions:**
    - Explain the use of lambda functions, which are anonymous functions in Python.
    - **Example:** Create a lambda function to square a number: square = lambda x: x**2.
- **Map, Filter and Reduce functions:**
    - **Map:** Applies a function to each item in a list.
    - **Filter:** Filters items in a list based on a condition.
    - **Reduce:** Reduces a list to a single value using a cumulative function.
- **Practical Example:** Use map to double the values of a list, filter to keep only even numbers and reduce to calculate the product of the numbers in a list.
- **Practical Exercise:** Create a list of numbers and use lambda functions with map, filter, and reduce to perform data manipulation operations.

4.8. Practical Integration Exercises

Propose exercises that require the combined application of the algorithms and control structures learned.

1. **Temperature Recording System:** Create a program that records daily temperatures and allows you to calculate the weekly average, maximum and minimum temperature, using functions and conditional structures.
2. **Search and Sort Lists:** Implement a function to sort a list of names and another function to search for a specific name using binary search.
3. **Factorial and Fibonacci Calculator:** Implement recursive and with for functions to calculate the factorial and Fibonacci sequence, comparing the efficiency of each approach.

4. **Student Grade Analysis**: Create a program that takes a class's grades, calculates the average, identifies the student with the highest grade, and checks how many students were above average using filter and lambda.

4.9. Conclusion of the Chapter

Chapter 4 addressed the fundamental data structures and algorithms that are crucial for the development of artificial intelligence applications. Understanding how and when to use structures such as lists, stacks, queues, sets, and dictionaries is essential for efficient data manipulation, which is one of the pillars of working with AI.

Additionally, we explore common algorithms that operate in these frameworks, providing a solid foundation for implementing machine learning and data processing techniques. Mastering these frameworks and algorithms not only facilitates the implementation of AI solutions but also improves the efficiency and performance of systems, allowing them to handle large volumes of data effectively.

Throughout this chapter, readers have been equipped with the knowledge necessary to apply these frameworks in a practical way in their projects. With this foundation, we are ready to move on to the next chapter, where we will explore the development of AI algorithms, delving into techniques that allow the creation of intelligent and adaptive models.

Chapter 5: Introduction to Algorithm Development for Artificial Intelligence

5.1. What is an AI Algorithm?

Start by explaining the definition of an AI algorithm and how it differs from a traditional algorithm.

- **Definition of AI Algorithm**: An AI algorithm is a set of instructions that allows a system to process data, recognize patterns, and learn from experiences to perform tasks autonomously.
- **Differences from Traditional Algorithms**: While traditional algorithms follow strict rules, AI algorithms are more flexible and adaptive, relying on data to make decisions.
- **Common Examples of AI Algorithms**: Image recognition, natural language processing, and product recommendation.

5.2. Introduction to Supervised and Unsupervised Learning

Explain the concepts of supervised and unsupervised learning, the two main approaches to machine learning.

- **Supervised Learning**:
    - Definition: Algorithms that learn from labeled data, i.e., where the expected outcome is already known.
    - Examples: Classification of emails as spam or non-spam, recognition of handwritten digits.
- **Unsupervised Learning**:
    - Definition: Algorithms that learn from unlabeled data, detecting patterns and relationships without direct guidance.
    - Examples: Grouping customers based on purchasing preferences, data segmentation analysis.

- **Practical Exercise**: Identify and classify different everyday problems as supervised or unsupervised learning.

5.3. Concepts of Regression and Classification

Introduce the two main types of problems in supervised learning: regression and classification.

- **Regression**:
    - Explanation: Regression is used to predict continuous numerical values based on input variables.
    - Example: Predicting real estate prices based on characteristics such as size, location, and number of bedrooms.
- **Classification**:
    - Explanation: Classification is used to categorize data into discrete classes.
    - Example: Identifying emails as "spam" or "not spam".
- **Practical Exercise**: Create a list of everyday examples that involve regression and classification, and explain the reason for each classification.

5.4. Algoritmos Comuns de IA: K-Nearest Neighbors (KNN) e K-Means

Explain some introductory AI and machine learning algorithms, such as KNN and K-Means.

- **K-Nearest Neighbors (KNN)**:
    - Definition: A classification algorithm that ranks data based on the closest examples in the data space.
    - Example: Classify types of fruits based on color, weight, and size, considering known "neighbor" fruits.
- **K-Means**:

- - Definition: An unsupervised grouping algorithm that organizes data into groups (clusters) with similar characteristics.
  - Example: Grouping customers from a store into segments based on purchasing behaviors.
- **Practical Exercise**: Create a simplified algorithm in Python to group a list of numbers into two groups based on proximity of values.

5.5. Notions of Neural Networks

Introduce the concept of artificial neural networks, one of the most powerful techniques in AI.

- **What is a Neural Network?**: Neural networks are models inspired by the human brain, formed by layers of nodes (neurons) that process and transmit information.
- **Basic Structure**:
  - **Input Layer**: Where the initial data enters the network.
  - **Hidden Layers**: Where data processing and learning takes place.
  - **Output Layer**: Where the final result is generated.
- **Application Example**: Image recognition, where the neural network identifies objects in a photo.
- **Practical Exercise**: Ask the reader to draw a representation of a simple neural network with an input layer, a hidden layer, and an output layer, labeling each layer.

5.6. Fundamentals of AI Model Evaluation

Teach the importance of evaluating AI models by addressing basic performance metrics.

- **Why evaluate models?**: Evaluating models allows you to understand if the algorithm is accurate and reliable for the problem it is trying to solve.

- **Common Metrics**:
    - **Accuracy**: Percentage of correct predictions in relation to the total.
    - **Accuracy and Recall**: Used to evaluate classification models, especially on unbalanced datasets.
    - **Mean Absolute Error (MAE)** and **Mean Square Error (MSE)**: Used for regression models, measuring the deviation of forecasts from the actual values.
- **Practical Example**: Explain how to calculate the accuracy for a model that classifies images as "cat" or "dog".

5.7. Data Pre-processing

Explain how to prepare and clean data before applying AI algorithms.

- **Importance of Preprocessing**: Raw data can contain errors, missing values, and inconsistencies that affect the performance of algorithms.
- **Pre-processing techniques**:
    - **Normalization and Standardization**: Adjust values to a common range, helping to standardize model inputs.
    - **Missing Value Handling**: Replace missing values with mean, median, or other value.
    - **Categorical Data Coding**: Turning non-numeric data into numbers, such as converting "yes" and "no" into 1 and 0.
- **Practical Example**: Provide a short list of data with missing values and ask the reader to fill it in and normalize it.

5.8. Basic Implementation of an AI Model in Python

Introduce a basic example of AI implementation using Python to help readers get started with hands-on programming.

- **Tools Needed:**
    - Libraries: pandas for data manipulation, scikit-learn for basic AI algorithms.
- **Step by Step:**

1. **Data Import:** Loading data from a public file or dataset.
2. **Pre-processing:** Clean and organize the data.
3. **Data** Splitting: Separating data into training and test sets.
4. **Training and Evaluation:** Applying an algorithm (such as KNN) to train the model and evaluate performance with test data.

- **Practical Example:** Implement a KNN model to classify flower species using the scikit-learn dataset "Iris".

5.9. Integration Exercises

Propose exercises that challenge the reader to apply what they have learned throughout the chapter.

1. **Email Classifier:** Simulate a simple classifier that identifies emails as "spam" or "non-spam" using basic supervised learning.
2. **Customer Grouping:** Develop a grouping model to organize customer data based on age and average spend, utilizing K-Means.
3. **Detection of Anomalies in Temperature Data:** Implement an algorithm that detects out-of-average values in a series of temperatures, using a simple regression algorithm to estimate the expected value.

5.10. Conclusion of the Chapter

Chapter 5 offered a comprehensive introduction to the fundamental principles of developing algorithms for artificial intelligence, empowering the reader to understand the types of machine learning, such as supervised and unsupervised learning, as well as key problem approaches, such as regression and classification. These concepts are crucial for building models that can learn from and adapt to data effectively.

We explore essential algorithms, such as K-Nearest Neighbors (KNN) and K-Means, as well as artificial neural networks, which are fundamental to advancing AI. We also address the importance of proper data preparation and evaluation metrics, which ensure that AI models deliver accurate and reliable results.

This chapter has served as an essential starting point for the development of AI algorithms, providing the reader with a practical and theoretical foundation. In the next chapters, we will delve into the use of specific tools and libraries, allowing the reader to move on to more complex and dynamic projects in the area of artificial intelligence.

Chapter 6: Machine Learning and Its Applications

6.1. What is Machine Learning?

Start the chapter by defining the concept of machine learning and its importance within the field of artificial intelligence.

- **Definition**: Machine learning is a branch of artificial intelligence that empowers systems to learn from data, identify patterns, and make decisions without the need for explicit programming for each task.
- **Importance**: Machine learning is key to building models that can adapt to new information and continuously improve their performance.

6.2. Types of Machine Apprenticeship

Explain the different types of machine learning and their characteristics.

- **Supervised Learning:**
    - **Definition**: A method where the model is trained with a set of labeled data, i.e., each input is associated with a correct output.
    - **Examples**: Classification (such as image recognition) and regression (sales forecasting).
- **Unsupervised Learning:**
    - **Definition**: A method where the model is trained on unlabeled data, looking for underlying patterns and structures.
    - **Examples**: Clustering and dimensionality reduction.

- **Reinforcement Learning:**
    - **Definition:** A method where an agent learns to make decisions through interactions with an environment, receiving rewards or punishments.
    - **Example:** Games, such as chess or video games.

6.3. Machine Learning Algorithms

Introduce some of the most widely used algorithms in machine learning.

- **Linear Regression:** A simple method for modeling the relationship between variables.
- **Decision Trees:** Structures that model decisions based on conditions.
- **Support Vector Machines (SVM):** Algorithms used for classification and regression.
- **Neural Networks:** Models inspired by the functioning of the human brain, used primarily in complex tasks such as speech and image recognition.

6.4. Data Pre-processing

Discuss the importance of data preprocessing to the effectiveness of machine learning models.

- **Data Cleansing:** Removing duplicate data, handling missing values, and correcting errors.
- **Normalization and Standardization:** Techniques for scaling the data, ensuring that all attributes contribute equally to the model.
- **Data Splitting:** The practice of separating data into training and test sets to evaluate model performance.

6.5. Applications of Machine Learning

Explore some of the many practical applications of machine learning in different industries.

- **Health**: Early diagnosis of diseases through the analysis of medical data.
- **Financial**: Detection of fraud in transactions and prediction of market trends.
- **Marketing**: Analysis of consumer behavior for segmentation and personalization of campaigns.
- **Transportation**: Autonomous vehicles that utilize machine learning for navigation and decision-making.

6.6. Implementing a Simple Model

Conclude the chapter with a practical example of how to implement a machine learning model using Python and a popular library such as Scikit-learn.

- **Data Import**: Using a dataset, such as the Iris set for flower classification.
- **Pre-processing**: Cleaning and preparation of data.
- **Model Training**: Creating and training the model with labeled data.
- **Evaluation**: Measurement of the model's performance using metrics such as accuracy.

Conclusion of Chapter 6

Chapter 6 provided a comprehensive overview of machine learning, one of the pillars of contemporary artificial intelligence. By exploring its definitions, types, algorithms, and practical applications, readers have gained a solid understanding of how machine learning works and its importance in various industries.

The concepts of supervised, unsupervised and reinforcement learning have been detailed, offering a clear view of how different approaches can be used to solve varied problems. Introduction to fundamental algorithms such as linear regression, decision trees, and neural networks provides readers with a starting point for implementing practical models.

Additionally, the chapter emphasized the importance of data preprocessing, a crucial step in ensuring that machine learning models are accurate and efficient. By learning how to clean, normalize, and slice data, readers are better prepared to handle real-world datasets, which is vital for success in AI projects.

Finally, by presenting a practical example of implementing a simple model in Python, the chapter not only reinforced the theory but also encouraged practice, allowing readers to apply what they learned in a practical context.

With this knowledge in hand, readers are ready to move on to more complex and specialized topics in the field of machine learning. The next step in this journey will be to delve into advanced techniques and explore how AI can be integrated into innovative solutions, preparing them to become protagonists in the evolution of technology.

Chapter 7: Neural Networks and Deep Learning

7.1. What are neural networks?

Start the chapter by defining the concept of neural networks and their analogy with the human brain.

- **Definition**: Neural networks are computational models inspired by the structure of the human brain, composed of layers of nodes (neurons) that process information and learn from data.
- **Importance**: They are the foundation of deep learning, enabling the modeling of complex relationships in large volumes of data.

7.2. Structure of a Neural Network

Describe the basic architecture of a neural network, including its core components.

- **Neurons**: Basic elements that perform calculations and transmit signals.
- **Layers**:
    - **Input Layer**: Receives the input data.
    - **Hidden Layers**: Process data through weights and activation functions.
    - **Output Layer**: Produces the final result of the network.
- **Weights and Bias**: Explain how weights adjust the importance of inputs and the role of bias in modeling.

7.3. Activation Functions

Explain activation functions and their importance to neural networks.

- **Definition**: Functions that determine the output of a neuron based on its inputs.

- **Examples of Functions**:
    - **Sigmoid**: Common in older neural networks, but can cause the problem of "gradient fading".
    - **ReLU (Rectified Linear Unit):** Widely used in deep networks due to its efficiency.
    - **Softmax**: Used in multiclass classification problems.

7.4. Neural Network Training

Cover the process of training a neural network, including the key steps.

- **Forward Propagation**: How data is passed through the network to generate a forecast.
- **Loss Calculation**: Measuring how far the forecast is from the actual value.
- **Backward Propagation**: The process of adjusting the weights through the backpropagation algorithm, minimizing the loss function.

7.5. Deep Learning

Define the concept of deep learning and how it relates to neural networks.

- **Definition**: A subfield of machine learning that uses deep neural networks (with multiple hidden layers) to model complex data.
- **Applications**: Image recognition, natural language processing, gaming, and more.

7.6. Tools and Libraries for Neural Networks

Introduce some of the top tools and libraries used to build neural networks.

- **TensorFlow**: One of the most popular libraries, developed by Google, for building and training deep learning models.
- **Keras**: A high-level API that runs on top of TensorFlow, simplifying the process of building neural networks.
- **PyTorch**: A library developed by Facebook, widely used in research and academia due to its flexibility.

7.7. Implementing a Simple Neural Network

Conclude the chapter with a practical example of how to implement a simple neural network using Keras and TensorFlow.

- **Data Import**: Using a dataset such as MNIST for digit recognition.
- **Model Construction**: Definition of the network architecture, including layers and activation functions.
- **Compilation and Training**: Configuration of the model and training with the data.
- **Evaluation**: Measurement of network performance using a test dataset.

Conclusion of Chapter 7

In this chapter, readers were introduced to the world of neural networks and the concept of deep learning. Understanding the structure and functioning of neural networks, along with the training process, provides a solid foundation for building models that can solve complex problems in a variety of areas.

Introduction to available tools and libraries simplifies access to neural network creation, encouraging experimentation and practical application of the concepts learned. The practical example of implementing a neural network with Keras and TensorFlow provides a valuable opportunity for readers to see how to apply the theory in a real project.

Chapter 8: Natural Language Processing (NLP)

8.1. What is Natural Language Processing?

Start the chapter by defining the concept of Natural Language Processing and its relevance in the interaction between humans and machines.

- **Definition:** NLP is a field of artificial intelligence that focuses on the interaction between computers and humans through natural language, enabling machines to understand, interpret, and respond to text or speech in a meaningful way.
- **Importance:** NLP is critical for building applications that facilitate communication and analysis of textual data, such as chatbots, machine translators, and recommendation systems.

8.2. Components of Natural Language Processing

Describe the main components and steps of NLP.

- **Tokenization:** The process of breaking down a text into smaller units, such as words or phrases, for analysis.
- **Syntactic Analysis:** The structuring of language in sentences and the identification of relationships between words.
- **Semantic Analysis:** The understanding of the meaning of words and phrases in context.
- **Disambiguation:** The process of determining what meaning a word has in a given context.

8.3. NLP techniques

Explain some of the techniques and methods used in NLP.

- **Language Models**: Algorithms that learn to predict the next word in a sequence based on previous words. Examples include n-gram models and recurrent neural networks (RNNs).

- **Sentiment Analysis**: A technique used to determine the emotion or opinion contained in a text, often applied in the analysis of consumer opinions and product feedback.

- **Named Entity** Extraction: Identification and classification of text entities, such as people, organizations, and locations.

8.4. Applications of Natural Language Processing

Explore some of the many practical applications of NLP.

- **Chatbots and Virtual Assistants**: Systems that interact with users through natural language, providing customer support and task automation.

- **Machine Translation**: Systems that translate text or speech from one language to another, such as Google Translate.

- **Text Analytics**: Tools that help analyze large volumes of textual data for insight extraction, such as survey reports and customer feedback.

- **Automatic Summarization**: Systems that generate concise summaries of long texts, making it easier to digest information.

8.5. NLP Tools and Libraries

Introduce some of the main tools and libraries used for natural language processing.

- **NLTK (Natural Language Toolkit):** A popular Python library that provides tools for working with text, including tokenization, parsing, and more.
- **spaCy:** An efficient and fast NLP library that supports multiple languages and is used in production applications.
- **Transformers:** A library developed by Hugging Face, which allows the use of advanced language models, such as BERT and GPT, for NLP tasks.

8.6. Implementing an NLP Example

Conclude the chapter with a practical example of how to implement a simple NLP task using NLTK or spaCy.

- **Data Import:** Loading a set of text data (e.g., product reviews).
- **Tokenization and Analysis:** Application of tokenization and syntactic analysis techniques to understand the structure of the text.
- **Sentiment Analysis:** Implementing a simple model to classify opinions as positive, negative, or neutral.
- **Display of Results:** Presentation of results in a clear and understandable way.

Chapter 8 Conclusion

In this chapter, readers have been introduced to the fascinating field of Natural Language Processing (NLP) and its importance in communication between humans and machines. Understanding NLP components such as tokenization, syntactic parsing, and semantic analysis gives you a solid foundation for handling texts effectively.

Exploring NLP techniques and applications has demonstrated how this area can be applied in a variety of contexts, from chatbots to sentiment analysis and machine translation. Introduction to available tools and libraries makes it easy to access the development of practical NLP solutions.

The practical example of implementing an NLP task provides readers with the opportunity to apply the concepts learned in a real project, strengthening their understanding and skills. With this knowledge, readers are ready to explore more advanced and innovative topics within the field of Natural Language Processing, contributing to the development of increasingly intelligent and useful systems.

Chapter 9: Computer Vision

9.1. What is Computer Vision?

Start the chapter by defining the concept of computer vision and its importance in the field of artificial intelligence.

- **Definition**: Computer vision is a subfield of artificial intelligence that allows machines to interpret and understand the visual world, processing images and videos to extract meaningful information.
- **Importance**: Computer vision is critical in applications ranging from facial recognition to medical image analysis to autonomous navigation.

9.2. Main Components of Computer Vision

Describe the essential components and steps of computer vision.

- **Image Acquisition**: The process of capturing images through cameras or sensors.
- **Image Processing**: Methods for enhancing and manipulating images, such as filtering, contrast adjustment, and noise removal.
- **Image Analysis**: Feature extraction and interpretation of the data contained in the images, including segmentation and edge detection techniques.

9.3. Computer Vision Techniques

Explain some of the techniques and approaches used in computer vision.

- **Object Detection**: Methods for identifying and locating objects in an image. Examples include Haar Cascades and YOLO (You Only Look Once).
- **Facial Recognition**: Techniques that allow the identification and verification of individuals based on their facial features.

- **Image Segmentation:** The process of dividing an image into significant parts for easy analysis. This can include segmentation by color, shape, or texture.
- **Convolutional Neural Networks (CNNs):** A type of neural network specially designed to process data with a grid structure, such as images, which have become fundamental in computer vision.

9.4. Applications of Computer Vision

Explore some of the many practical applications of computer vision in a variety of industries.

- **Image Recognition:** Use on social media platforms to identify faces in photos.
- **Automatons and Autonomous Vehicles:** Systems that use computer vision to detect obstacles and navigate complex environments.
- **Medicine:** Analysis of medical images, such as X-rays and MRIs, to aid diagnoses.
- **Industry and Manufacturing:** Inspection of product quality through automated cameras that detect defects.

9.5. Tools and Libraries for Computer Vision

Introduce some of the key tools and libraries used to develop computer vision applications.

- **OpenCV (Open Source Computer Vision Library):** One of the most popular libraries for image processing and computer vision, which provides functions for image manipulation and analysis.
- **TensorFlow and Keras:** Used to implement convolutional neural networks and other deep learning techniques in computer vision.

- **PyTorch**: Another powerful library that is widely used in computer vision research due to its flexibility and ease of use.

9.6. Implementing a Computer Vision Project

Conclude the chapter with a practical example of how to implement a simple computer vision task using OpenCV.

- **Data Import**: Loading a test image.
- **Image Processing**: Application of filtering and edge detection techniques.
- **Object Detection**: Using a pre-trained model to identify objects in the image.
- **Results Display**: Presentation of the original image and the processed image, highlighting the detected objects.

Conclusion of Chapter 9

In this chapter, readers were introduced to the field of computer vision and its importance in a variety of modern applications. Understanding the essential components such as image acquisition, processing, and analysis provides a solid foundation for developing computer vision solutions.

The exploration of the techniques and applications demonstrated how computer vision can be used to solve real problems, from face identification to medical analysis. Introduction to available tools and libraries, such as OpenCV and TensorFlow, facilitates access to the development of practical projects in this area. The practical example of implementing a computer vision task provides readers with the opportunity to apply the concepts learned in a real project, reinforcing their understanding and skills. With this knowledge, readers are ready to explore more advanced topics in computer vision, contributing to the development of innovative and intelligent systems that can transform the way we interact with the visual world.

Chapter 10: Ethics and Final Thoughts in Artificial Intelligence

10.1. The Importance of Ethics in Artificial Intelligence

Start the chapter by defining ethics in the context of artificial intelligence and why it is a crucial aspect to consider.

- **Definition of AI Ethics**: AI ethics refers to the set of principles and standards that guide the development and implementation of artificial intelligence technologies, aiming to ensure that their applications are fair, responsible, and respect human rights.

- **Importance**: As AI technologies become more integrated into everyday life, their social, economic, and political implications require a careful ethical approach to avoid negative consequences.

10.2. Ethical Challenges in Artificial Intelligence

Describe some of the key ethical challenges faced in the development and use of AI.

- **Bias and Discrimination**: AI can perpetuate or even amplify existing biases if the training data contains bias. Examples include facial recognition systems that fail to correctly identify individuals from minority groups.

- **Data Privacy and Security**: The collection and analysis of large volumes of data raises concerns about users' privacy and the security of personal information.

- **Transparency and Explainability**: Many AI solutions function as "black boxes," making it difficult to understand how decisions are made. This is especially critical in areas such as medicine and criminal justice.

- **Responsibility and Accountability**: In the event of an error or failure of an AI system, it is essential to define who is responsible—the developer, the company, or the machine itself.

10.3. Guidelines for the Ethical Development of AI

Present some guidelines that can be followed to ensure the ethical development of AI systems.

- **Fairness:** Ensuring that AI systems are designed to be fair and non-discriminatory, involving diversity in data collection and model development.

- **Transparency:** Implementing practices that make AI decision-making processes more understandable, allowing users to understand how and why decisions are made.

- **Privacy:** Adopting strict data protection measures and ensuring that users have control over their personal information.

- **Accountability:** Establish clear accountability frameworks that attribute the consequences of decisions made by AI systems to individuals or organizations.

10.4. The Future of Artificial Intelligence

Explore the future prospects for artificial intelligence and the ethical implications that may arise.

- **Technological Advancements:** Discussion of how advancing AI can transform industries, improve efficiency, and create new employment opportunities, but it also presents ethical challenges as machines become more autonomous.

- **Human-Machine Collaboration:** The importance of developing a healthy balance between automation and human interaction, ensuring that AI complements human skills rather than replacing them.

- **Regulation and Policies:** The need for a clear regulatory framework to guide the development and use of AI by promoting ethical practices and protecting the rights of individuals.

10.5. Final Considerations

Conclude the chapter and e-book by reflecting on the reader's journey through the content presented.

- **Learning Summary**: Reaffirm the importance of the fundamentals of programming, machine learning, natural language processing, and computer vision, as well as emphasize the relevance of ethics in all AI applications.
- **Inspiration for the Future**: Encourage readers to continue their exploration in the area of artificial intelligence by applying not only their technical skills but also an ethical conscience to their projects.
- **Call to Action**: Inspire readers to be proactive in contributing to a future where artificial intelligence is developed and used responsibly and ethically, benefiting society as a whole.

Chapter 10 Conclusion

In this chapter, readers were introduced to the importance of ethics in artificial intelligence, addressing the challenges that arise with the use of these technologies and the guidelines necessary for their responsible development. As AI continues to evolve and integrate into society, ethical consideration becomes increasingly essential.

The guidelines discussed provide a clear path for the ethical development of AI systems, emphasizing fairness, transparency, privacy, and accountability. As we look to the future, it is crucial for both AI developers and users to adopt an ethical stance towards the technologies they create and utilize.

Material Extra

Term	Definition
Algorithm	A set of instructions or rules defined to solve a problem or perform a specific task.
Sentiment Analysis	Natural Language Processing (NLP) technique that identifies and classifies opinions or sentiments expressed in a text, such as positive, negative, or neutral.
Big Data	Extremely large and complex data sets that cannot be easily managed or analyzed using traditional methods.
Classification	A machine learning problem where the goal is to categorize data into pre-defined classes or groups based on specific characteristics.
CNN (Convolutional Neural Network)	A type of neural network designed to process data with a grid structure, such as images. Used in computer vision tasks.
Deep Learning (Aprendizado Profundo)	A subfield of machine learning that uses deep neural networks to learn multi-layered representations of data.
Disambiguation	The process of identifying what the correct meaning of a word or phrase is in a given context.

Term	Definition
Data Engineering	The process of preparing and transforming data so that it can be used by machine learning and artificial intelligence algorithms.
Framework	A set of tools and libraries that provide a development framework to make it easier to build applications, such as TensorFlow and PyTorch.
Natural Language Generation (NLG)	A subfield of NLP that focuses on creating text or speech in a way that is understandable and natural to humans.
Hyperparameters	Parameters defined before training a machine learning model, which control the learning process and affect the performance of the model.
AI (Artificial Intelligence)	The simulation of human intelligence processes by computer systems, including learning, reasoning, and self-correction.
General AI	A theoretical concept of artificial intelligence that would have the ability to perform any cognitive task that a human can perform.
Weak AI	AI systems designed to perform specific and limited tasks, such as virtual assistants and chatbots.
Logic	A branch of philosophy and mathematics that studies principles of valid reasoning. In programming, logic is fundamental for the construction of algorithms.

Term	Definition
Machine Learning Model	A mathematical or computational representation of a problem, created from training data.
NLP (Natural Language Processing)	A field of AI that enables machines to understand, interpret, and generate human language in a meaningful way.
Forecast	The act of using a machine learning model to estimate future outcomes based on historical data.
Neural Network	A computational model inspired by the structure of the human brain, composed of interconnected neurons that process information.
Regression	A type of machine learning problem that involves predicting a continuous value based on input data.
Image Segmentation	The process of dividing an image into significant parts or regions for analysis, often used in computer vision.
Model Training	The process of teaching a machine learning model using a set of training data, adjusting its parameters to minimize errors.
Transfer Learning (Aprendizado por Transferência)	A technique in machine learning where a model trained on one task is reused as a starting point for a model on a different task.
Computer Vision	A field of AI that allows machines to interpret and understand the visual world, processing images and videos to extract meaningful information.

Term	Definition
Z-Score	A statistical measure that describes the position of a value relative to the mean of a group of values, often used in detecting anomalies in data.

This table provides a clear and organized view of the fundamental terms and concepts related to logic and artificial intelligence.

References and Recommended Readings

Books

1. **"Artificial Intelligence: A Modern Approach"** - Stuart Russell and Peter NorvigOne of the most complete and respected books in the field of AI, it covers everything from the fundamentals to advanced applications.

2. **"Deep Learning"** - Ian Goodfellow, Yoshua Bengio, and Aaron CourvilleThis book is an essential reference for understanding deep learning, covering both theory and practices.

3. **"Python Machine Learning"** - Sebastian Raschka and Vahid MirjaliliA practical guide that teaches you how to implement machine learning algorithms in Python.

4. **"Pattern Recognition and Machine Learning"** - Christopher M. BishopA comprehensive book that offers a detailed introduction to pattern recognition and machine learning.

5. **"Programming in Haskell"** - Graham HuttonAn excellent introduction to programming logic using the Haskell language, which emphasizes functional programming.

Articles and Papers

1. **"The Ethics of Artificial Intelligence"** – Nick Bostrom and Eliezer Yudkowsky, an article that discusses the ethical implications of AI and the importance of considering ethics in its development.

2. **"Attention is All You Need"** - Ashish Vaswani et al.
   This article introduces the Transformer model, which has revolutionized natural language processing.

Online Resources

1. **Coursera - Machine Learning by Andrew Ng**
   Coursera Machine Learning
   A free and highly recommended course for beginners in machine learning.

2. **edX - Introduction to Computer Science and Programming Using Python**
   edX Python CourseAn introductory course that covers programming logic and basic programming concepts.

3. **Kaggle**
   Kaggle
   A platform for data science and machine learning competitions, where you can practice and learn from real datasets.

4. **Towards Data Science**
   Towards Data Science
   A Medium blog that features articles on AI, machine learning, and data science, accessible and written by professionals in the field.

Communities and Forums

1. **Stack Overflow**
   Stack Overflow
   A developer community where you can ask questions and find answers about programming and AI.

2. **Reddit - r/MachineLearning**
   Reddit Machine Learning
   An active community of machine learning enthusiasts and professionals who share news, research, and projects.

3. **AI Alignment Forum**
   AI Alignment Forum
   A space for discussion on AI alignment and ethical issues related to the development of intelligent systems.

Downloadable Python Code Samples

1. Basic Programming Logic

- **Description:** A simple example of programming logic that demonstrates conditional structures and loops.

- **Código:** Download: logica_programacao.py

```python
# Exemplo de Lógica de Programação: Números pares e ímpares
for i in range(1, 11):
    if i % 2 == 0:
        print(f"{i} é um número par")
    else:
        print(f"{i} é um número ímpar")
```

2. List Manipulation

- **Description**: Code that shows how to manipulate lists in Python, including addition, removal, and iteration.
- **Código**: Download: manipulacao_listas.py

```python
# Exemplo de Manipulação de Listas
numeros = [1, 2, 3, 4, 5]
numeros.append(6)   # Adiciona um número
print(numeros)

numeros.remove(2)   # Remove um número
print(numeros)

# Iteração sobre a lista
for numero in numeros:
    print(f"Número: {numero}")
```

3. Machine Learning: Sorting with Scikit-learn

- **Description**: A basic example of classification using the Iris dataset and the KNN algorithm.

- **Código**: Download: classificacao_iris.py

```python
# Exemplo de Classificação com Scikit-learn
from sklearn.datasets import load_iris
from sklearn.model_selection import train_test_split
from sklearn.neighbors import KNeighborsClassifier

# Carregando o conjunto de dados
iris = load_iris()
X = iris.data
y = iris.target

# Dividindo os dados em conjuntos de treino e teste
X_train, X_test, y_train, y_test = train_test_split(X, y, test_size=0.2, random_state=42)

# Treinando o modelo
modelo = KNeighborsClassifier(n_neighbors=3)
modelo.fit(X_train, y_train)

# Avaliando o modelo
precisao = modelo.score(X_test, y_test)
print(f"Precisão do modelo: {precisao:.2f}")
```

4. Natural Language Processing: Sentiment Analysis with NLTK

- **Description:** An example of sentiment analysis using the NLTK library.
- **Código:** Download: analise_sentimentos.py

```python
# Exemplo de Análise de Sentimentos com NLTK
import nltk
from nltk.sentiment import SentimentIntensityAnalyzer

# Baixando o pacote necessário
nltk.download('vader_lexicon')

# Analisando sentimentos
analisador = SentimentIntensityAnalyzer()
texto = "Eu amo programação! É tão gratificante."

resultado = analisador.polarity_scores(texto)
print(f"Resultado da análise de sentimentos: {resultado}")
```

5. Computer Vision: Edge Detection with OpenCV

- **Description:** An example of edge detection in an image using the OpenCV library.

- **Código:** Download: deteccao_bordas.py

```python
# Exemplo de Detecção de Bordas com OpenCV
import cv2

# Carregando a imagem
imagem = cv2.imread('caminho/para/imagem.jpg', cv2.IMREAD_GRAYSCALE)

# Aplicando detecção de bordas
bordas = cv2.Canny(imagem, 100, 200)

# Mostrando a imagem com bordas
cv2.imshow('Bordas', bordas)
cv2.waitKey(0)
cv2.destroyAllWindows()
```

Conclusion

In this eBook, we explore the fundamentals of programming logic with a special focus on its application in the field of artificial intelligence. From basic logic concepts to advanced machine learning techniques, the content has been structured to provide a comprehensive understanding of the essential skills needed for anyone looking to enter this ever-evolving field.

We hope that the practices presented, the code examples and the recommended resources have been useful for your learning. The journey into the field of programming and artificial intelligence can be challenging, but also extremely rewarding. Keep practicing, experimenting, and learning, and you'll find new opportunities and possibilities to apply your skills.

Thanks

We thank everyone who contributed to the realization of this e-book. First of all, a special thanks to the authors and researchers whose works served as a reference and inspiration for this content. His dedication to the field of artificial intelligence and programming is critical to the advancement of knowledge.

We also thank the educators and professionals in the field who shared their experiences and teachings, helping to shape the future of new programmers and AI experts.

Finally, a thank you to you, the reader, for investing your time and energy in learning and growing. We wish you much success in your journey in programming and artificial intelligence!

About the Author

 Paulo Fagundes is an information technology professional with senior experience in Artificial Intelligence and Software Development. He has a strong background in programming logic and machine learning, having worked on several projects that combine technological innovation and practical solutions.

Currently, Paulo is Chief AI Officer (CAIO) at MakeAI Innovations, where he leads artificial intelligence development initiatives. He also serves as GenAI/Security Lead Prompt Engineer, AI Research Scientist, Master Machine Learning Engineer, and Data Engineer. In addition, he is the owner of the CodeXpert AI profiles on X and Instagram, where he shares insights and resources on programming and AI.

With a passion for teaching and sharing knowledge, Paulo is always on the lookout for new ways to demystify complex concepts, making them accessible to everyone. He believes that education is the key to the future, especially in the field of technology, where adaptation and continuous learning are essential.

You can connect with Paulo and follow his work through his LinkedIn profile: Paulo Fagundes

www.ingramcontent.com/pod-product-compliance
Lightning Source LLC
Chambersburg PA
CBHW070128230526
45472CB00004B/1466